Dogs and Birds Book 1:
Supplementary Notes and Lesson Plans for Parents and Teachers

Elza and Chris Lusher

© 2007 Elza and Chris Lusher
Illustrations © 2006 Liz Patton
Revised fifth printing 2012
Website: www.dogsandbirds.co.uk

The material in this book should not be reproduced by any means,
including photocopying, without the permission of the authors
Published by Dogs and Birds
ISBN 978-0-9568497-4-8
ISMN 979-0-9002217-4-2

Printed by Kingsley Print and Design Limited, Egham, Surrey

Contents

Section 1 – The Basic Elements of the Dogs and Birds Approach 1
   Introduction 1
   Teaching Dogs and Birds 2
   Using These Supplementary Notes 3
   Lesson Times 4
   The Importance of Daily Practice 4
   Small Animal Tiles and Coloured Staves 5
   Use of the Blank Notes Edition 6
   Using a Manuscript Book 7
   Using the Animal Stickers 7
   A Suitable Keyboard 8

Section 2 – The Components used in the Seventeen Steps 9
   Rhythm Exercises 9
   Musical Pieces 9
   Sung Finger Exercises 10
   The Echo Game 11
   Small Animal Tiles/Wooden Animals 12
   Combining the Echo Game with the Animals and Staves 13
   Stories 14
   Improvisation 14
   Composition 15
   Balancing the Elements 15

Section 3 – The Seventeen Steps 17
   STEP 1 17
   STEP 2 20
   STEP 3 22
   STEP 4 23
   STEP 5 24
   STEP 6 25
   STEP 7 26
   STEP 8 28
   STEP 9 30
   STEP 10 32
   STEP 11 33
   STEP 12 34
   STEP 13 36
   STEP 14 37

STEP 15 39
STEP 16 40
STEP 17 41
Section 4 – Some Helpful Tips to Make Things Easier, in Particular for the Very Young Child 42
   Further use of the Small Animal Tiles and Coloured Staves 42
   Using the Coloured Staves on the Piano in Place of the Score 43
   A Variation on the Listening Game for the Very Young 43
   Various Techniques to Help with Rhythm 43
   Helping the Child by Pointing out Notes with Your Fingers 44
   Walking on the Staves 45
   An Alternative Order for the Pieces in Book 1 45
   The Transition From Animal Notes to Blank Notes 46
   Bringing a Toy Animal or Doll to Visit the Animals 47
   A Copying Game 47
   Playing the Echo Game without Notation 48
   Another Variation on the Listening Game and the Echo Game 48
   Making use of New Technology 49
Section 5 – Important Notes for Parents 50
   Hand Position and Posture 50
   Musical Notation 51
      The Names of the Notes 51
      Beats and Note Lengths 51
      The Octave 52
      The Musical Staves and the Clefs 52
      Bar Lines 53
      Repeat Marks 53
      First and Second Time Bars 53
      Da Capo al Fine 53
Section 6 – Additional Explanatory Notes for Teachers 54
   Rests and Time Signatures 54
   Quavers 54
   Finger Numbers 54
   Group Teaching 54
Section 7 – CD Tracks and Credits 55

Section 1 – The Basic Elements of the Dogs and Birds Approach

Introduction

Dogs and Birds is a method which makes it possible to teach the piano/keyboard to children as young as three years old very successfully. It is *not* necessary for the child to know the alphabet. The method is also advantageous for older children since it dramatically speeds up the learning process and builds musicality. It can be used successfully for children up to the age of seven years old. There is a strong emphasis on singing whilst playing the keyboard – the method has its roots in the immensely successful approach to teaching children developed by the Hungarian Zoltán Kodály. As well as learning to play the piano/keyboard, the child will be able to sing and have a very solid foundation for further musical study.

The following resources are available from www.dogsandbirds.co.uk:
- Dogs and Birds Books 1 and 2 (in both Animal Notes and Blank Notes Editions)
- Dogs and Birds: Nursery Rhymes and Famous Melodies (in both Animal Notes and Blank Notes Editions)
- Supplementary notes to Book 1 (these notes)
- A CD of the pieces and rhythm exercises in Book 1, included with these notes
- A set of small animal tiles and coloured staves
- A set of wooden animals and a large set of staves
- A manuscript book (with either 4 staves per page or 6 staves per page)
- A sheet of animal stickers (containing 7 sets of the 7 animals plus a few extra animals)
- A complete music set for beginners (with either small animal tiles or wooden animals).

This method is suitable for teaching children from three to seven years old, although in some cases even younger children may learn successfully. In general, the animal notes editions of the books are recommended for ages three to six and the blank notes editions are recommended for ages six to seven. Very often the two editions are best used in parallel.

Teaching Dogs and Birds
There are a number of ways to teach children using the Dogs and Birds approach and materials. One option is to arrange private piano lessons from a sympathetic teacher from the outset. However many parents might not wish to do this initially, especially if their children are very young. Some of these materials have been prepared in order to allow parents to work with (or teach) their children, even if they have had no previous musical experience.

It is possible for parents to teach the material in Book 1 to their children. Studying in this way will provide an enjoyable but strong musical foundation for those wishing to learn any instrument, including the piano. Book 2 is aimed at those wishing to continue their study of the keyboard or piano. The material in Book 2 is more advanced and for this it is really necessary to have lessons from a piano teacher. Of course if the parent has a solid background in the piano it might be possible to teach the material in Book 2 as well.

The principle behind this method is very simple for children to understand. This means that they can actually practise unaided between lessons. This is especially important for those of a young age. It makes lessons worthwhile since without daily practice the child might well forget melodies, rhythms and even the notes from one week to the next.

The CD, which contains all the pieces and rhythm exercises in Book 1, is extremely important for a parent who is teaching his/her child – especially those parents without any previous musical background. The appropriate tracks must be listened to before each lesson. The CD can also be used to help the child with his/her practice. You should try to copy the material on the CD as closely as possible. It is particularly important for the child always to sing, and not to play too fast. Please use the CD as a guide.

Using These Supplementary Notes
These notes are written in order to help you get the most from working through Dogs and Birds Book 1. The material has been broken up into 17 "Steps". The term *steps* has been used rather than *lessons* since the amount of time needed for each step depends on the age and application of the child. Each step might take a few lessons or just one.

Each step consists of a set of exercises and games to play with the children to help them to learn the concepts. Since the exercises in the steps are often similar, the appropriate techniques will be explained in this introduction before detailing the various steps. The exercises are ordered differently in each step so as to add variety to the lessons. The method involves:
- Marching and "tapping" the rhythm exercises in Book 1
- Playing and singing the musical pieces in Book 1
- Sung finger exercises, not included in Book 1
- Playing an echo game involving singing and pitch recognition
- Using the small animal tiles or wooden animals, and staves in various ways, including combining them with the echo game
- Making up stories about the illustrations in the book
- Improvising, by using the whole body and moving freely on the keyboard
- Simple composition, when the child is ready, possibly using the tiles and staves

Sections 2 and 3 should definitely be followed by parents who wish to teach their children, but teachers may also find them useful. Section 2 describes how to carry out the musical exercises and games, and section 3 contains the steps.

Section 4 gives a set of ideas which may help if children are having problems with particular aspects of the approach. These tips can be especially useful for extremely young children.

Section 5 contains material written specifically for parents who have no previous musical experience. It explains the simple musical notation used in Book 1, shows how you can use animals to help find the notes on the piano keyboard and shows (with reference to Book 1) how these notes can be represented using musical notation. *Those without prior musical experience should read section 5 before working through section 3 (and the ideas in section 4) with their child.*

Section 6 contains notes for teachers, explaining some of the principles behind this approach and section 7 gives more information about the CD.

Lesson Times
Typically a session with the child might last 30 minutes. This may seem a long time for a three, four or five year old to concentrate on one thing, however by breaking up each lesson into a series of smaller parts you will find that this amount of time is necessary – the time will fly by. Each step usually has five or six parts to it. It is recommended that you give the child enough time to master each step before going onto the next. There is no benefit to be gained from rushing the child – learning music should be an enjoyable and fun experience. In some cases, if parents are teaching their children at home, it might be better to split the lessons into shorter sessions, especially initially if the child's concentration span is short.

The Importance of Daily Practice
At this age short but *daily* practice is much more important than a longer period less frequently. You should find that with 5 minutes every day (both singing and playing the pieces) the child will improve rapidly. You will see that the child's concentration span will increase noticeably.

Practice should be planned but varied. Each day the child should sing and play at least 2 pieces twice, and perform 2 elements of the step (for example rhythm exercises and improvisation, "tapping" and the echo game, or composition and finger exercises).

Small Animal Tiles and Coloured Staves
The 56 small tiles with animal pictures on them, can be placed either on the keyboard in the appropriate position or on the set of coloured staves. The back of the tiles are black so they can be turned over on the staves once the child knows the note. The treble clef and top lines on the staves are coloured red, and the bass clef and bottom lines are coloured blue. This is to help the child distinguish between the left and right hand. Generally you can mark the child's left and right hands in various ways, for example use a coloured marker to put a red spot on the right hand and a blue on the left, or make use of coloured ribbons or coloured elastic bands.

The tiles can be used for many different musical learning games, as will be explained in these supplementary notes:
- The tiles bring extra fun to the lesson and practice, and make learning notes even easier for the child. They can be turned over onto the black side as the child learns the note.
- Each set contains 7 sets of the 7 animals (Cat, Dog, Egg, Fish, Goose, Ant, Bird) plus an extra Cat, an extra Ant, an extra Bird and 4 extra Dogs.
- The tiles can be used from the first lesson, when the child needs to find all the Dogs on the keyboard.
- Together they help the child to learn the geography of the keyboard. There is an animal tile for every white key on a full-sized keyboard.
- They can be used for making up finger exercises, using the coloured staves.
- They help the child to realize that an animal can sit anywhere horizontally on a particular line.
- They can help with echo games, composition, improvisation, memory games, sight-singing, sight-reading and learning the position of the notes on the staves.
- There are enough animals to compose interesting tunes or to copy songs from book 1 onto the staves.

- Each tile contains an animal character from the Nursery Rhymes and Famous Melodies book. All the characters are different, and children love to pick out which is which.

You can use Blu-Tack (or an equivalent adhesive putty) to stick the animal tiles onto the staves. The staves can be placed on the piano in place of a musical score, enabling the child to play the melody he/she has composed using the tiles.

The front cover of the staves shows the positions of the animals on the keyboard for the notes below and including middle-C, and shows the position of the animals on the lines of the bass clef. The back cover shows the positions of the animals on the keyboard for the notes above and including middle-C, and shows the position of the animals on the lines of the treble clef. The staves therefore act as a useful reminder for both student and parent.

Use of the Blank Notes Edition
The blank notes edition can either be used on its own, or in parallel with the animal notes edition. It depends to some extent on the child. Some children (in particular the older ones) wish to learn from the blank notes edition. It is still vitally important that the child sings the animal names of the notes as he/she plays in order to develop the inner ear. With younger children you can use the two editions in parallel and this should be encouraged. You can place both books in front of the child on the piano. Ask him/her to play a piece from the animal notes edition and subsequently to try to play the same piece from the blank notes edition. Do not remove the other book – it will act as a safety net. Another approach, which is sometimes useful, is to get the child to work through the animal notes edition and later on work through the blank notes edition.

In group teaching with mixed ability students it is possible for them to play the same piece together, with the stronger students using the blank notes edition.

Using a Manuscript Book
It is very important to keep a record of your lessons, and the easiest way to do this is to use a manuscript book. Here you can summarize the material covered lesson by lesson. It is much easier to keep track of what the child has learned and how well he/she is progressing by writing it down clearly.

You should always write into the manuscript book the rhythm exercises, pieces, finger exercises, and echo games etc. that the child should practice during the following week or days.

Later on you can use the manuscript book for writing down compositions or other written homework.

Manuscript books are available from www.dogsandbirds.co.uk with either four or six staves per page. Use the four stave manuscript book when studying Book 1.

Using the Animal Stickers
The animal stickers have been produced in the main for giving to the child as a reward for good work during lessons. The stickers are small enough to be stuck on the keys as an aid to learning. This is *not* a practice to be encouraged however, especially for children of 5 and over, who are usually quite capable of remembering the appropriate names of the keys easily. It can be tried with children under 5 to make the lessons more fun initially, but you should stop the practice as soon as it is possible. It could potentially slow down the child by developing a reliance on seeing the sticker in order to recognize the key. Sometimes it is necessary to use the stickers in this way, but they should only be used as an aid if the child is really having problems remembering.

If you do not have a set of small animal tiles, the stickers can be stuck onto card to create extra musical notes to use with the keyboard or the large set of staves.

A Suitable Keyboard
Since singing is an important part of this approach it is vital to have an instrument that is in tune. For the material in Book 1 a three to four octave keyboard is perfectly adequate. An electric keyboard will be perfectly in tune and therefore very suitable to sing with. If you would like to start teaching your three or four year old child to play the keyboard you might not initially wish to spend a lot of money to buy an instrument. At the present time the keyboards obtainable from music shops start at around £70-£80 and you might not wish to spend that sort of money. These instruments tend to be "all-singing, all-dancing", with many different instrument sounds and rhythms. These are good but somewhat unnecessary for teaching young children the basics of the keyboard. If you wish to see whether your child is interested in playing, you can probably find something cheaper by looking around. You might be able to find some good second-hand bargains.

Section 2 – The Components used in the Seventeen Steps
Rhythm Exercises
These exercises are dispersed throughout the book. It is quite common for very young children (under five years old) to find these harder than the musical pieces. However they are very important for the children in order to develop a strong sense of the beat, and they are excellent preparation for playing the musical pieces hands together. They really should not be overlooked. There are a number of ways the exercises can be carried out and you will find instructions in the steps below. They should *not* be carried out too fast. Something like one beat (one crotchet/quarter note) per second is ideal. A good way of "tapping" the rhythms is to get the child to use his/her palms to play many notes at once on the keyboard – low notes with the left hand and high notes with the right hand. Play from the shoulder – this is very good for freeing up the arms. The child should count the beat aloud "One Two Three Four etc." whilst "tapping". Use the CD as a guide if required.

Very young children often struggle initially with co-ordination in the rhythm exercises. They find it difficult to play different rhythms in the two hands. Many have difficulty distinguishing between left and right, and top and bottom. These problems can be solved by marking the top line of the exercises with a red pencil and the bottom line with blue. You can then make a little red mark on the child's right hand and a blue mark on the left hand with marker pens, or put red and blue rubber bands or ribbons around his/her wrists. This should make a big difference.

If the child still has difficulty then the teacher or parent should try tapping the top or bottom line while the child taps the other line. In this case you should COUNT together.

Musical Pieces
Please read the "Notes for Teachers" on the inside back cover of Book 1 before starting to play the pieces. It is essential that the child sings the melody whilst playing the pieces and you should always encourage this. You should start by singing the melody before playing (if

possible) and get the child to sing with you. If you have difficulty in sight-singing a piece then first listen to the CD in order to familiarize yourself with it, and then play the melody on the keyboard whilst singing it. The child might be reluctant to sing at first. However if you persevere with this, especially if you always sing as well each time a new melody is introduced, the child should become quite confident within a few lessons and happily sing on his/her own. The child should always begin each piece by counting in one bar as is done on the CD.

Usually young children find it difficult to sing the G or F below middle C (see section 5 for an explanation of the musical notation). If this is the case then you might ask the child to sing the melody an octave higher than written. Listen to "Aquarium" (track 39 of the CD) for an example.

Sung Finger Exercises
These additional exercises are important in that they:
- prepare the child for playing the pieces;
- provide good ear-training;
- improve the child's singing ability;
- strengthen the fingers;
- introduce the geography of the piano;
- prepare for improvisation or composition.

Since these exercises are not printed in Book 1 you should write them out in the manuscript book, in order to keep track of where you are. If the child cannot yet read or write you may need to draw animal symbols to symbolize the notes. As well as using the exercises in these notes, you can also make up your own. The small animal tiles and coloured staves can be used for composing simple finger exercises, as described later.

Make sure that the child can play through each exercise before attempting to play the piece that follows. The child should play from the shoulders – moving his/her whole arm as a unit. In order to see how this should be done ask the child to draw a series of arches (like a viaduct) on top of the keyboard, hands separately. The child's arms should be free, without any tension. Children have a tendency to raise their shoulders and keep their elbows close in to their waists. Therefore please ensure that the child keeps his/her elbows away from the body, with the shoulders down. For fun you can mention that the child should play as if he/she has hedgehogs under his/her arms which mustn't be harmed. Also make certain that the child does not just play from the elbow or wrist – the movement should start from the shoulder. Each note should be detached and not played legato (smoothly). The wrists should not be dropped (to allow space for a mouse to run under the hands).

The child should always sing the animal names out loud whilst playing. Throughout these supplementary notes upward facing stems on minims and crotchets are used to signify notes to be played with the right hand and downward facing stems signify notes to be played with the left hand. These exercises should be played at each octave on the keyboard, with the child always singing at the octave which is most comfortable for him/her (probably around middle C). If the keyboard has many octaves then the child should play these exercises in a standing position and walk along the piano in order to reach the required notes. Sing with the child in order to encourage him/her.

It is good practice to ask the students to try playing the finger exercises with their eyes closed. This will allow them to feel the spacing of the notes on the keyboard and help them ultimately to look at the music, rather than relying on looking at their hands whilst playing.

The Echo Game
The echo game involves playing notes at random on the keyboard and asking the child to identify which is which, singing them back using the animal names. If you have a set of small animal tiles or wooden animals (see below) you should always use them as you play the echo game (as described later). An example of the echo game is shown in step 2. There you are asked to play Dogs and Birds randomly. You should play the notes in a number of different octaves in order to train

the child's ear, although the child should always sing the pitch that is comfortable for him/her. Gradually in the steps that follow more notes are added. Relatively quickly you should find that the child is able to distinguish between the different notes. Really occasionally children find this challenging, especially once the number of notes increases. If this is the case you might wish to start with the child simply singing or humming the notes back before identifying them by name.

If the child has problems with this game at the beginning then try another way to train the ear. Play two "Dogs" of different pitches and ask the child to identify which note is high and which is low. You can do similar exercises as you add more notes. Always make sure that the child can hear whether notes are moving up or down before you start to introduce difficult sequences.

Small Animal Tiles/Wooden Animals

As well as the small animal tiles, a set of wooden animals is available for use with this method, as is a large set of staves. Each set contains one of each of the seven animals. The animals can be placed on either the keyboard or the large staves. For the exercises in the seventeen steps you can use either small animal tiles or wooden animals. You should ask the child to place the animals in the correct place on the keyboard or the staves. You can call each stave a shelf, staircase, or a block of flats, for example, or you can tell the child that 𝄞 symbolizes a house in the mountains and 𝄢 a house in the valley. Another way is to liken the top stave to five red benches and the bottom to five blue benches in a school. Some children need to sit on red benches, others on blue. And some need to stand between the benches.

It is particularly important that you do the exercises with the animals and staves since if the child is using the animal notes edition it is possible for him/her to play the music by looking at the animals without actually realizing on what line or space a particular animal sits. You can also use animals and staves as you play the echo game. This is very good both for ear training and visualization of the notes, and it helps to make learning more interesting.

You can watch examples of animals and staves in use in the Musical Exercises and Games section of the Video Demos at www.dogsandbirds.co.uk, and also on the Dogs and Birds Piano Method YouTube channel at www.youtube.com/user/elzalusher.

When you have introduced all of the notes you can play a game with a dice. Place an animal on the stave then roll the dice and based on the result get the child to add the appropriate animal in its correct position. It is good to ask the child to sing the animal name at the correct pitch then check it by playing the note on the piano. A throw of 1 corresponds to the same animal, 2 to the next animal note etc.

Combining the Echo Game with the Animals and Staves
We take as an example the exercises in step 2, where the child is introduced to the Dog and the Bird. You should sit at the piano and get the child to sit in front of the open staves. Play and sing "Dog Bird Dog" and ask the child to echo this by singing it back. Then play either Dog or Bird and ask the child to identify it. He/she should recognize which note you have played and sing it back with its appropriate name and pitch. At the same time he/she should put the correct animal in its proper place on the staves. Now again play either Dog or Bird. The child should sing the appropriate animal name and pitch and either place the correct animal on the staves or remove it if it is there already. If you are using the tiles then just place another animal on the staves. Continue the game by playing randomly either Dog or Bird. This is extremely good for ear training and also for teaching the child the correct positioning of the notes on the staves.

If the child has difficulty with this game initially you can try a simpler version of this exercise. First place the Dog and Bird in their correct positions on the staves. Then play Dog and Bird randomly and ask the child to point at the appropriate animal (either with a stick or a pencil) as they sing its name. Once the child can do this then you can progress to the harder version of the game.

If you find that the child can do this exercise easily then you can try playing Dog or Bird one octave higher or lower. Always ask the child to sing back at the pitch most comfortable for him/her (probably that closest to middle C).

You can also build up sequences of Dog and Bird. For example play "Dog Dog Bird Bird Dog Dog Bird" and ask the child to sing the phrase back with the appropriate names, pointing to the correct animal as he/she sings. The level of difficulty of the sequences you can use will depend on the child. Try to challenge him/her somewhat, but not too much. Make sure that the child can master the challenge.

Continue with the game in a similar manner as you add more notes. Finally the child will be able to remember and sing back 4 to 6 note melodies and point to the notes while singing.

Stories
Each piece in the book has a title and is illustrated. In general the animals in the illustrations are the same as those in the musical notes, although there are a few exceptions. Please make up stories with the child using the illustrations as a guide. This helps to stimulate further the interest and imagination of the child and makes the lessons more fun and enjoyable. It is very advantageous to talk about the illustrations since it brings the child closer to the pieces and the music.

Improvisation
For some time during each lesson the child should be allowed to express himself/herself on the keyboard, by "playing" a story. This is the time when the child can bang on the keyboard freely, or stroke it softly depending on the story he/she makes up. It is also an excellent time for the child to have a break and stand up from the piano stool and stretch his/her body. The story could perhaps describe the child's favourite fairy tale, a game with his/her pet or friends – practically any

aspect of his/her life. In the first few steps some ideas are given. You should help by suggesting themes, but make sure this activity is kept under control. Keep a strict time limit. Make sure the child uses a great variety of sounds and touch – for example soft or loud, long or short, single notes or groups of notes, hands together or separately, smooth or detached, etc.

Composition
In addition to these exercises and games the child will sometimes be asked to compose a short piece under your guidance. Try to compose music similar to that which the child has already learnt, or use the sung finger exercises as a basis for the composition. This is an excellent use for the small animal tiles and coloured staves. Children can write out their compositions using the animals and staves and then place the staves on the piano to play.

Balancing the Elements
All the elements discussed in this section are important for the child in order to become a rounded musician. In general children will be better at some elements than others. If, for example, tapping the rhythm exercises is weak, playing the musical pieces hands together is difficult, or carrying out the listening games is hard do not worry. Practise, watch the child, and use your imagination to make the particular element more interesting.

If something is complicated or hard for the child try to solve it from a different angle. Please do not force anything! For example, if the child is reluctant to sing initially then you should sing continuously and ask him/her to copy you or just sing along with you. If the child has difficulty with rhythm then try many different ways to achieve your goal – use pieces of paper or names of vehicles to describe lengths of notes, try marching, clapping or barking, or other techniques as outlined in these notes. If the child's hand position is weak then you should first determine if he/she is ready for a proper hand position, or whether it is just better to play with index fingers (possibly with an open hand) or thumbs. Maybe start to do preparatory work away from the piano to achieve the correct hand position – ask the child to hold his/her head with curved fingers or to hold his/her hands like a tiger's claws.

The most important thing is to motivate your child. And each child is different so you will need to find out what works in each particular case. For some making the lessons fun is the most important thing. In other cases you can fire his/her imagination by telling stories. You might use finger puppets to help with your descriptions. For others it will be necessary to fill your lessons with kindness, loving care and friendship. You should always make sure that your child will be successful so give exercises that will be challenging but possible, and make the lessons varied. Work together with your child to produce a happy, stimulating and successful lesson.

Section 3 – The Seventeen Steps

STEP 1

Improvisation – Before you open Dogs and Birds you should explain to the child that music is wonderful for expressing feelings and moods, and it can describe many different pictures and stories. In order to demonstrate this you should do the following improvisation exercises and get the child to repeat them.

First play LOW, LOUD, LONG notes – these represent the *elephant*. Do this with your hands, playing many notes simultaneously – first one hand and then the other, as if you are walking side to side on the bass notes.

Now walk all the way up the keyboard softly. These SOFT, LONG notes increasing in pitch represent a *cat* walking. At the very end hit your hand hard on LOW BASS notes to illustrate the cat jumping down from the fence it has been creeping along. You can then do a similar thing on the black keys as well, representing a *black cat*.

You can describe happy *birdsong* by playing HIGH, LOUD, SHORT notes. Do this by turning your hands with a rotary motion from the wrists. Play with the backs of your hands – both hands simultaneously, using a rocking movement.

Listen to track 1 of the CD for examples of these first three improvisation exercises.

Finding the First Note – When the student is ready, turn to page 1 of the book and ask him/her to find all the Dogs on the keyboard. Put a Dog tile (or pencil) on top of each of these Dogs – you need one tile/pencil for each of the Ds on the keyboard. If you are using the toy wooden animals then place the wooden Dog on each of the Ds in turn. Get the child to play the notes with the thumbs, and sing "Dog". Make sure that all the fingers are above the keyboard, and curved if the child is ready for that. If the child is under 4 years old, then it may be easier to use the index fingers rather than the thumbs.

Sung Finger Exercise – Ask the child to play:

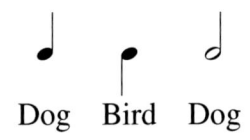

$$\text{Dog} \quad \text{Bird} \quad \text{Dog}$$

Use the right hand thumb/index finger to play the Dog and the left hand thumb/index finger to play the Bird. Remember that the child should play from the shoulders, moving his/her whole arm – the child should not just play from the elbow or wrist. It is important that the child sings "Dog Bird Dog" whilst playing the notes. You should perform this exercise at each octave on the keyboard, but always sing around middle C i.e. the pitch that is most comfortable for the child. There is an example of this on track 1 of the CD.

Musical Pieces (Page 3) – First sing "Playground" together with the child using the animal names i.e. Dog Dog Bird Bird Dog Dog Bird etc. If necessary listen to the CD first and then play the melody on the keyboard whilst singing it. Parents without previous musical experience should see "Important Notes for Parents" (section 5 of these notes) for advice and instruction. If the child is very young and has no experience of reading from left to right then hold a pencil together and point out the notes as you sing. This will teach the child to read and helps with concentration.

After singing the line then get the child to play and sing. Repeat the same procedure with "By the Lake". The child should possibly use his/her thumbs to play these notes – the right-hand thumb for the Dog and the left-hand thumb for the Bird. The child should play from the shoulders – moving the whole arm. Advice on a proper hand position is given in section 5.

Rhythm Exercises (Page 2) – These are the first rhythm exercises. Rhythm exercises are dispersed throughout the book and they are very important for the child in order to develop a strong sense of the beat. The child and teacher/parent should march, clap and count the first three rhythms. Marching helps the student to feel an even beat. Most of the rhythm exercises have four beats in a bar, so the child and teacher/parent should count "1 2 3 4 | 1 2 3 4 | 1 2 3 4 |...". As you clap try to emphasis the first beat of each bar.

Using Cars to Explain the Lengths of Notes – If the child has difficulty understanding the lengths of the notes then use the chart on the back cover of Book 1 in order to aid understanding. A car takes up less space in a car park than a bus. The black notes (crotchets/quarter notes) have a length of one beat, the white notes with stems (minims/half notes) last for two beats, and the white notes without stems (semibreves/whole notes) last for four beats. The same applies to notes when they are written on a musical stave. If the child is unable to count then ask him/her to clap or tap the rhythm on the back of the book, whilst saying aloud the words:
"Car Car Car Car | Big-Car Big-Car | Car Car Big-Car | Very-Very-Big-Bus".

You should use these words with the children in the rhythm exercises (especially with extremely young children), until they are ready to count using numbers. Further suggestions for teaching very young children are given in section 4.

STEP 2

Rhythm Exercises (Page 4) – In this and the remaining rhythm exercises the child should "tap" the rhythms and count the beat using numbers (or cars if necessary). This should be done by striking the keys with open palms as described before, in section 2. Hand symbols indicate which hand should be used. If a note is written directly above another note then the notes should be played (or tapped) at the same time. If the beat is not yet even the child and teacher/parent should march as in step 1 until the beat becomes strong. It is a good idea to listen to a clock ticking and ask the child to count to the ticks.

Sung Finger Exercise – Sing and play:

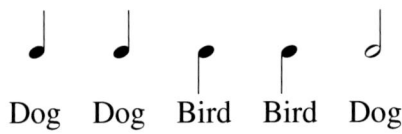

Dog Dog Bird Bird Dog

Play this at each octave on the keyboard as described earlier, always singing (at a comfortable pitch). If possible once the child has played this ask him/her to play it again with his/her eyes closed.

Stories – Never miss an opportunity to make up stories about the illustrations. For example in "In the Bush" and "Cotton Flower" (page 6) you can talk about the nest, which is being prepared for the next new note (the Egg). Try to make up a 3 to 5 sentence story about building a soft nest in the bush. A story always enables the child to find links that help the learning process.

Musical Pieces (Pages 5 and 6) – Play and sing "Empty Sack", "Wait until it is Dark", "In the Bush" and "Cotton Flower". Do this in a similar manner to earlier, that is singing first and then playing and singing.

The Echo Game – Now play the echo game. This involves playing Dogs and Birds at random on the keyboard and asking the child to identify which is which and sing them back using the animal names. Remember to play these notes in a number of different octaves.

Small Animal Tiles/Wooden Animals – Get the child to put the animals in their correct places on the keyboard and then place them on the appropriate places on the staves. It is often easier for the child if you call the stave a ladder or stairs. The Dog lives on the top (or red) ladder and the Bird lives on the bottom (or blue) ladder – or the Dog lives in a mountain home and the Bird lives in a house in the valley.

The animals and staves can be linked with the echo game to provide an excellent opportunity for ear training. Get the child to place the Dog and the Bird on the staves. Play and sing "Dog", then play and sing "Bird". After that play just one of them and ask to child to identify it by removing the appropriate note from the staves. Then play a note again. Ask the child to identify it, either by removing a note from the staves or putting it back on the staves in its appropriate place. With practice the child will soon be able to distinguish notes with ease. This game can be extended to more notes later.

Improvisation – Ask the child whether he/she can think of a story to describe by playing on the keyboard. If not suggest a theme for the child to improvise. You could try to express different moods, for example being happy, sad, sleepy, angry, lively etc.

Composition – If you have the animal tiles and coloured staves make up a simple melody using the notes you already know and then sing it as you play it on the piano.

STEP 3

Improvisation – Make up a new story and play it on the keyboard. This time the student should use both hands whilst playing or should play together with the parent/teacher. Play LOUD and SOFT notes, and LONG and SHORT notes. Together with the child think of situations when you need to be LOUD or QUIET and describe them using the piano.

Sung Finger Exercise – Sing and play:

♩ ♩ ♩ 𝅗𝅥

Dog   Egg   Dog   Bird

Stories – Look at the picture on page 7 and discuss it with the child. Why must the animals behave during the concert? What is a concert?

Musical Pieces (Page 7) – Sing and play "Promise to Behave".

Small Animal Tiles/Wooden Animals – Use the animals Dog, Bird and Egg to teach the child their positions on the keyboard and the staves. Maybe link this with the echo game as described in the previous step.

Rhythm Exercises (Page 8) – Tap these rhythms with alternate hands counting aloud as you do so. Please do not forget to march if it is still necessary.

Musical Pieces – In "Egg and Spoon Race" (page 9) you can ask the child to count "1 2 3 4 | 1 2 3 4 | 1 2 3 4 | …" rather than singing the animal names as he/she plays this piece. Sing and play page 10. If the child is ready then use the second (index) finger for Egg. Make sure that the index finger is curved if possible. Please do not force this below the age of 5 or 6. Only use the right hand for "Far-off Hills" and "Egg Rock". Do not play anything smoothly (legato) – play separated notes using the whole arm.

STEP 4

Stories – Talk about the pictures with the child. The Dog is looking for the Egg in the secret garden, when there is a full moon. Can he find the Egg there? No, the Egg is amongst the hills. In this and in all cases make the pieces more interesting by talking about the stories in the pictures.

Musical Pieces – Sing and play "When the Moon is Full" and "The Secret Garden" (page 11), and "Golden Rings" (page 13).

The Echo Game – Play the echo game with Dog and Egg. Maybe also introduce Bird occasionally. As before play the note and ask the child to identify and sing it.

Small Animal Tiles/Wooden Animals – Use the animals once more, placing them in turn on the keyboard and the staves. Again link this exercise with the echo game. Place the Dog, the Egg and the Bird on the staves initially. Play and sing these three notes in turn. Now play a single note and ask the child to identify the note as explained in step 2. Repeat with other notes. Try to challenge the child gradually.

Rhythm Exercises (Page 12). Tap numbers 1, 2 and 3.

Improvisation – Make up another story. A possible story is about a snake climbing up a tree to catch a bird at the top. The bird in the tree is the same as in the first lesson. Is the bird caught by the snake or does it escape? Slide your arm along the keys, moving up the keyboard, pressing down as you do so. What happens next will depend on your answer. Then get the child to repeat this story.

Sung Finger Exercise – Sing and play:

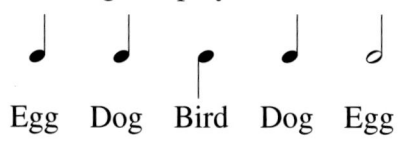

Egg   Dog   Bird   Dog   Egg

Now try to repeat it with your eyes closed.

STEP 5

Musical Pieces – Sing first and then play and sing "Rug from Morocco" (page 13) and "The Forest Comes Alive" (page 14).

Sung Finger Exercise – Sing and play:

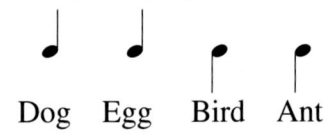

$$\text{♩} \quad \text{♩} \quad \text{♩} \quad \text{♩}$$

Dog   Egg   Bird   Ant

using the thumbs for Dog and Bird and the index fingers for Egg and Ant. Please use curved index fingers if possible. Play with detached notes, using your arms. Alternatively you could make up your own finger exercise using Dog, Egg, Bird and Ant.

Musical Pieces – Sing and play "Desert" (page 14) using the second finger of the left hand (curved if possible).

Improvisation – Make up a story or use the following one. A frog is jumping happily at the lakeside. A fish calls her for a secret meeting the following day. They meet at 3 o'clock and they swim together to the bottom of the lake where they investigate the hidden treasure that the fish had found earlier.

The Echo Game – Play the echo game with Bird and Ant. Possibly add Dog as well. Do not make this too difficult. Combine this with the small animal tiles or wooden animals if you have them.

Stories – Talk about the pictures on pages 15, 16 and 17. The Dog invites her friends for an adventure. She leads them through the open gate to go to the mountain in order to see the wonderful sky.

Musical Pieces – Play "A Safe Path" (page 15) with the left hand only. Use detached notes, because in general at this stage the child's fingers and hands are not yet strong enough to play legato.

Rhythm Exercises – Tap page 12, number 4 and page 16 numbers 1 and 2.

STEP 6

The Echo Game – Play the echo game with Bird, Ant and Dog. Maybe add Egg as well, if the child can distinguish the notes easily. If not then make it as simple as possible. Use Dog and Bird plus one other animal (Egg or Ant).

Sung Finger Exercise – Sing and play:

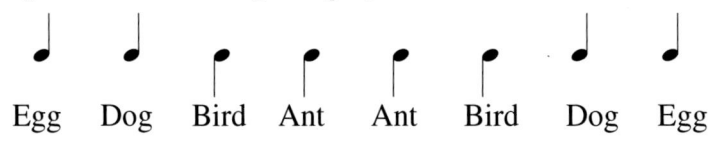

| Egg | Dog | Bird | Ant | Ant | Bird | Dog | Egg |

Rhythm Exercises – Tap page 16 numbers 3 and 4.

Stories – Continue discussing the pictures on pages 16 and 17. The animals are now out in the mountains. Possibly they will stay out all night. It is very clear in the mountains and they can see the Milky Way in the sky.

Musical Pieces – This time ask the child to try to sing "Open Gate" (page 15) before playing it. If he/she has difficulties with this then use the piano to check the notes. Also try this with "Watch the Milky Way" and "Great Smoky Mountain" (page 17).

Small Animal Tiles/Wooden Animals – Use the tiles or wooden animals. Find their places on the keyboard and on the staves. Link this with the echo game, if you haven't done so already.

Improvisation – Make up your own story or you can improvise a story about a lost baby Kangaroo. If you like, you can use the titles of the pieces in the book to give you ideas for stories.

Composition – Using the animal tiles (or by drawing animals in the manuscript book) make up a melody using Egg, Dog, Bird and Ant. The child should then play and sing it on the piano. Ask the child which notes he/she can remember, then turn these over to the black side and get him/her to play and sing it again.

STEP 7

Stories – "Trick on You" is a hard piece. It is tricky because there are no long notes where the child can rest. There is no time to wonder. You should concentrate now! The Dog is doing a trick with the cards.

Musical Pieces – Sing and play "Stop Your Wondering" and "Trick on You" (page 18).

Sung Finger Exercise – With the addition of a new note (the Goose), the five notes the child now knows form a *pentatonic scale*. Using both hands play and sing:

♩	♩	♩	♩	♩
Egg	Dog	Bird	Ant	Goose

If the child is ready then get him/her to use the middle (3rd) finger for the Goose (curved if possible). Make sure that the child still uses detached notes and uses the whole arm.

Musical Pieces – Using only the left hand play and sing "Picnic Basket" and "Somersault" (page 19).

Rhythm Exercises – Tap page 20 numbers 1 and 2.

Composition or Improvisation – Now you can start making up your own music in a more structured way. Make up your own rhythm of four bars in length. If it is possible you can write it down in the manuscript book. If the child is younger and not ready for this you can use the small animal tiles and coloured staves. Use the tiles with the black sides uppermost. For this purpose, you can place the tiles close together to represent crotchets/quarter notes and further apart to represent minims/half notes. If your child is not ready to do this yet, or particularly likes improvising, then ask him/her to think of a story to improvise. Or you could suggest a theme. You could try for example "Walking in a rainy day". You can use the music to describe raindrops (in the park or forest), your steps, your partner's steps (friend, parent or pet), thunder, heavy rain, a rain storm, and finally a rainbow and sunshine.

The Echo Game – Play the echo game with Goose, Bird and Dog. Possibly add Egg. Don't forget to use the wooden animals or tiles, and staves.

STEP 8

Rhythm Exercises – Tap page 20, numbers 3 and 4.

The Echo Game – Play the echo game with Goose, Bird, Dog and Egg. If the child finds this difficult then don't play all the notes in a single phrase. Just play two different notes at a time. [For example play Dog Bird, then Dog Egg, then Egg Dog, followed by Bird Bird Goose Goose.] You should always introduce the notes to the child before playing any melody. For example play and sing Egg Dog Bird Goose and ask the child to sing this phrase twice before starting the game. Repeat this throughout the game before playing each sequence of notes.

Composition or Improvisation – Compose a new rhythm and add a melody to it (using either the manuscript book or animal tiles and staves), or improvise a story based on the child's favourite activity.

Musical Pieces – Sing and Play "Take Your Partner" and "Sunday Afternoon" (page 21), and "Stepping Stones" (page 23). Once again please talk about the illustrations in order to make the pieces even more interesting for the child. Now the animals are having a party on Sunday afternoon. Who was the Dog's partner before the Goose? Possibly it was the Bird. That is why she is resting (or sleeping) now. The semibreve/whole note is used for the first time in "Sunday Afternoon".

Sung Finger Exercise – Play with hands *together* and sing the *left* hand notes:

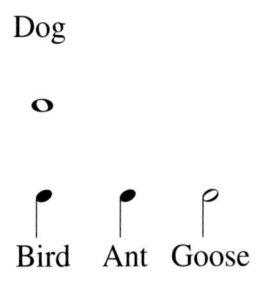

      Dog

      o

    ♩   ♩   ♩
    Bird   Ant   Goose

The right hand should play the Dog at the same time as the left hand plays the Bird.

This and the next few sung finger exercises will help the child to prepare for playing musical pieces with *hands together*.

Small Animal Tiles/Wooden Animals – Do not forget to use the tiles or wooden animals. You can use the animals and the staves to help with the composition, or you can link them with the echo game as usual. You can also make up other ways to use the tiles and staves to help with the child's score reading.

STEP 9

Rhythm Exercises – Clap or tap the rhythm exercises on page 22 SLOWLY with an EVEN beat. Please make sure that the third beat is *not* longer than the others. The "dot" following a note increases its length by half as much again. Therefore a dotted minim/half note has a length of 3 beats rather than 2.

Composition – Get the child (with your help) to make up his/her own rhythm with 3 beats in a bar and write it down (maximum 6 bars long). Either write this in the manuscript book or use the small animal tiles and coloured staves as earlier.

Sung Finger Exercise – Play hands together and sing the *right* hand part:

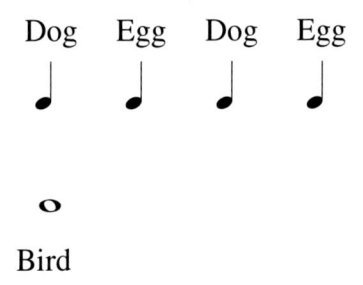

Dog	Egg	Dog	Egg
♩	♩	♩	♩

o

Bird

The left hand should play the Bird at the same time as the right hand plays the first Dog. Hold the Bird down for four beats.

Musical Pieces – Sing, then sing and play "Wheelbarrow" (page 23), "Tea Time" (page 24) and "Forbidden City (Page 25). Talk about the pictures as before. Our friends have now arrived in China to visit the Emperor. Their appointment is in the Forbidden City. They just have time to taste some Jasmine tea before their meeting.

The Echo Game – Play the echo game with Goose, Ant and Bird. Maybe you can combine this with the tiles or wooden animals here, but still focus on singing.

Improvisation – This can now be made more structured. The phrase

Goose Dog Goose Dog Bird

can either be repeated as an echo or changed to become an answer:

Goose Dog Goose Dog Goose

You can either play a "question" phrase and ask the child to provide the "answer", or ask him/her to devise both question and answer. Usually the question phrase is "open" and the answer phrase "closed" as below:

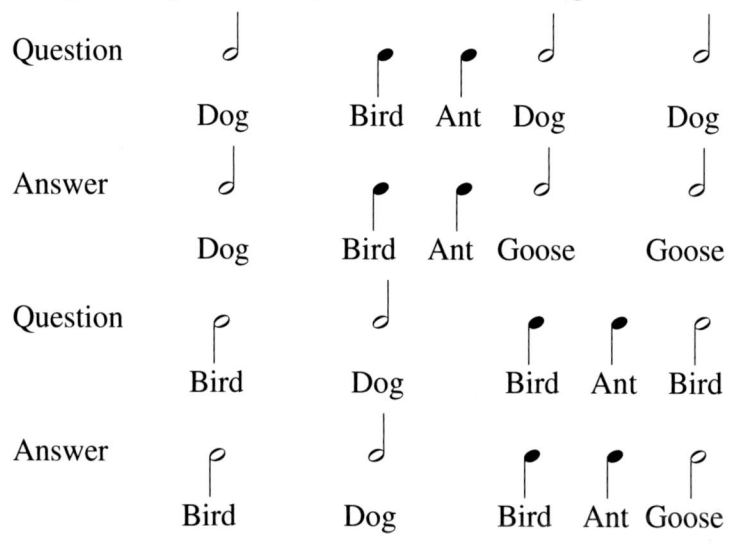

Question Dog   Bird Ant Dog   Dog

Answer   Dog   Bird Ant Goose Goose

Question Bird   Dog   Bird Ant Bird

Answer   Bird   Dog   Bird Ant Goose

The answer phases may differ from these.

STEP 10

The Echo Game – Play the echo game with Ant, Dog and Egg.

Composition – Get the child to make up a new rhythm in three beats and then add a simple melody to it.

Rhythm Exercises – Tap page 28, numbers 1 and 2.

Small Animal Tiles/Wooden Animals – Play with the tiles or wooden animals on the keyboard and staves. Use them for your composition and link them with the echo game.

Musical Pieces – Sing and play "Chinese Pagoda" (page 26). This has a complicated rhythm known as syncopation. The child must feel this syncopated rhythm as he/she counts or plays. To help with this initially you can just tap and count this piece or count the right hand melody, instead of singing the animals.

Musical Pieces (left hand only) – Play and sing the left hand parts of "Hands Together" and "Traffic Jam" (page 29).

Sung Finger Exercise – play with hands *together* and sing the left hand notes:

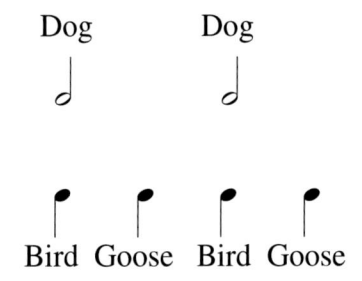

        Dog   Dog

Bird Goose Bird Goose

The right hand should play the Dogs at the same time as the left hand plays the Birds, since the Dogs are written directly above the Birds.

STEP 11

Musical Pieces – Play "Hands Together" and "Traffic Jam" (page 29) with both hands and sing the left hand part as you do this. Play and sing *only* the left hand part of "Welcome to My Home" (page 30).

Rhythm Exercises – Tap and count page 28, numbers 3 and 4.

Sung Finger Exercise – play with hands *together* and sing the left hand notes:

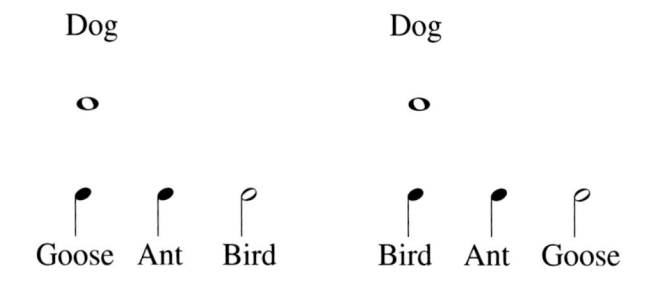

            Dog   Dog

Goose Ant Bird   Bird Ant Goose

If your child is willing to make up his/her own finger exercises then you should encourage this. Possibly you can combine use of the animals and staves, and the sung finger exercises at this stage.

The Echo Game – Play the echo game with Goose, Dog and Egg.

Small Animal Tiles/Wooden Animals – Place the tiles or wooden animals you have learnt up to now on the keyboard and on the staves. These are Goose, Ant, Bird, Dog and Egg. As you play the notes on the keyboard, ask the child to sing them back and place the correct animals on the appropriate place on the staves. The child must not forget to sing.

Musical Pieces – COUNT and play "Night after Night" (page 27). Be very careful with the beat in this piece. The 3rd beat must *not* be longer than the 1st and 2nd beats in each bar. Very young children are often not ready to keep an even beat with 3 in a bar. Learn this piece in 2 or 3 weeks time if your child has difficulty with it now.

STEP 12

Musical Pieces – Sing and play "Welcome to My Home" (page 30), adding the long "D". Then play "Dreamy Head" (page 30) both hands together and sing the left hand part.

Stories – You should discuss the picture on page 31. The Goose is taking the corn to the Winter Palace. Who is it for? For the Prince or Princess? Who lives in the palace? How far away is it? Why is it called the Winter Palace?

Musical Pieces – Play hands separately and sing "Winter Palace" and "Crush the Corn" (page 31). Sing the melody using the animal names or sing the beat numbers to the melody.

Rhythm Exercises – Tap page 32, numbers 1 and 2.

Sung Finger Exercise – Play hands together and sing the right hand part:

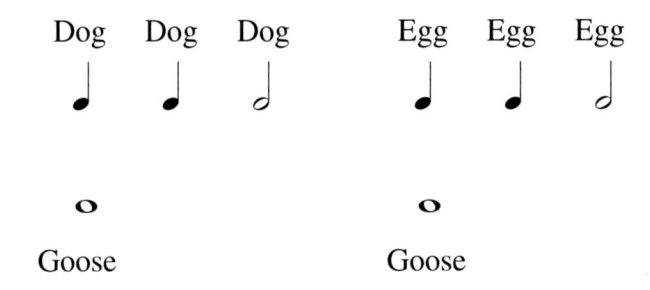

Dog Dog Dog	Egg Egg Egg
♩ ♩ ♩	♩ ♩ ♩
o	o
Goose	Goose

Use third fingers only all through the exercise. The Goose in the left hand should be played simultaneously with the first Dog and the first Egg in the right hand.

The Echo Game – Play the echo game with Goose, Ant, Bird and Dog, possibly using the wooden animals or tiles, and staves as earlier.

Small Animal Tiles/Wooden Animals – Use the tiles or wooden animals, getting the child to put them on the keyboard and the staves, and link this with the echo game.

Improvisation – This is probably the time to ask the child to improvise a structured melody. Use a "question and answer" approach. For example you might play:

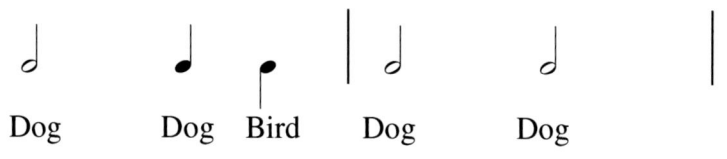

𝅗𝅥	𝅘𝅥 𝅘𝅥	𝅗𝅥	𝅗𝅥
Dog	Dog Bird	Dog	Dog

and the child might answer with:

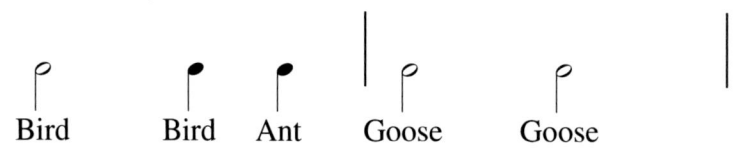

𝅘𝅥 𝅘𝅥 𝅘𝅥	𝅘𝅥	𝅘𝅥
Bird Bird Ant	Goose	Goose

If the child is not yet ready for this then ask him/her to improvise a rhythm clapping the "answer" to your rhythm "question" and/or you could just ask him/her to ECHO back exactly the same melody that you sung or played. Counting is a big help if difficulties occur.

STEP 13

Musical Pieces – Play "Winter Palace" (page 31) with hands *together* and sing the melody. Then do the same with "Crush the Corn" (page 31). Play "Jack and His Men" (page 33) with hands *separately* and COUNT.

Stories – Look at the picture on page 33. Who is Jack? Is he the boss? Which of the animals is the weakest, the strongest and the hardest worker?

Rhythm Exercises – Tap page 32, numbers 3 and 4.

Sung Finger Exercise – Play in a detached way and sing:

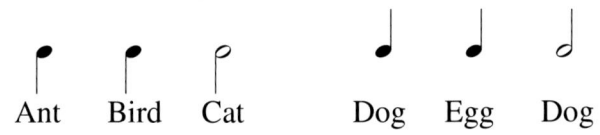

| Ant | Bird | Cat | Dog | Egg | Dog |

Small Animal Tiles/Wooden Animals – Place the appropriate tiles or wooden animals in their places on the keyboard and on the staves. Make sure that the child understands the middle C position and the continuity between the two staves.

The Echo Game – Play the echo game with Cat, Dog and Egg. You can link this with the wooden animals or tiles, and staves. If the child finds this easy then you play Cat Dog and Egg one octave higher or lower.

Musical Pieces – Sing first, then sing and play "Stick and Hat Stomp" (page 34). Make sure that the Cat is played with the left hand in this piece, as is indicated in the book.

Improvisation – Improvise a story on the keyboard or improvise a simple duet (with student and teacher/parent). Make sure you count together and play at the same tempo (speed). You can use melodies from the finger exercises and those you have used for the echo games. Please make it simple!

STEP 14

Musical Pieces – Play "Jack and His Men" (page 33) hands together and COUNT as you sing the left hand melody. After this try to sing the left hand melody without playing it but play the right hand part at the same time.

Musical Pieces – Play "Hop on My Back" (page 35) and "Floating By" (page 37). Approach these pieces in the following way. First play the parts hands separately i.e. sing and play the right hand part, then count and play the left hand part. Once both parts are known very well hands separately you can then ask the student to play them hands together. Always sing or count the melody when you play hands together.

If the child can sing the melodies very well then you can ask him/her to sing the melody (without playing it) whilst accompanying himself/herself with the left hand.

Rhythm Exercises – Tap page 36, numbers 1 and 2.

Sung Finger Exercise – Play and sing hands separately:

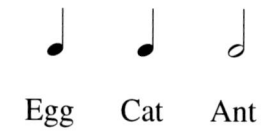

♩   ♩   ♩

Egg   Cat   Ant

First play this with the right hand at all octaves on the piano. Then repeat the same exercise using the left hand, again at all octaves on the piano. If this is easy then add the second hand as a semibreve/whole note, playing either Egg, Cat or Ant.

Small Animal Tiles/Wooden Animals – Use the tiles or wooden animals with the keyboard and staves.

The Echo Game – Play the echo game with Ant, Cat and Egg. Make sure to use the wooden animals or tiles, and staves.

Composition – Ask the child to compose a 4 or 6 bar rhythm for two hands. Help him/her to write the bar lines in first then fill in the bars. If he/she is too young to write then use white and black paper as described in section 4 of these notes.

STEP 15

Small Animal Tiles/Wooden Animals – Place the tiles or wooden animals on the keyboard and the staves as usual. Focus on both Fishes and both Geese.

Musical Pieces – Play "Old MacDonald" (page 38) and sing the animal names of the notes. "Da Capo al Fine" means go back to the beginning and end at "Fine" without the repeat.

Sung Finger Exercise – Play and sing:

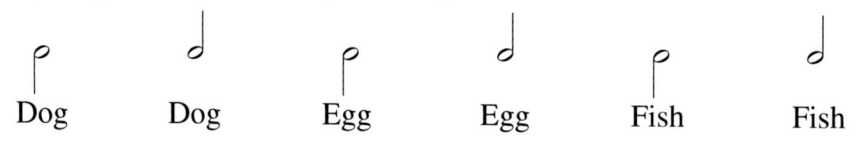

| Dog | Dog | Egg | Egg | Fish | Fish |

Here the notes played in the right hand (stems up) should be played an octave higher than those played in the left hand (stems down).

Composition – Compose a simple melody to go with the 4 or 6 bar rhythm written in step 14. Compose the melody for one hand only.

Musical Pieces – Sing and play "Aquarium" (page 39). If the child struggles with the low Fish then possibly he/she can sing the melody an octave higher, as on the CD. By this stage children often like to attempt to sing the low note even if they cannot quite make it – this is fine.

Musical Pieces – Approach "Wishing Well" (page 42) in the following way. Play each part hands separately, COUNTING whilst you play the right hand and SINGING the melody whilst you play the left hand. You will ask the child to play the piece hands together in step 16.

Rhythm Exercises – Tap page 36, numbers 3 and 4.

The Echo Game – Play the echo game in the bass clef with F, A and middle C. Possibly it is advisable to use the small animal tiles or wooden animals.

STEP 16

The Echo Game – Play the echo game with Cat, Dog, Egg and Goose. If the child is able to then you can try even more notes. Reinforce this by using the wooden animals or small animal tiles, and staves.

Musical Pieces – Play "Wishing Well" (page 42) hands together. Try this at first by counting as you play and then by singing as you play. Then play and sing "Transposition" (page 41). Make sure that the child understands that this is the same melody as in "Aquarium".

Rhythm Exercises – Tap page 40, numbers 1 and 2.

Sung Finger Exercise – Sing and play:

```
   ♩     ♩     ♩     ♩     ♩
  Cat   Bird  Ant  Goose  Fish
```

First play this with the left hand at all octaves on the piano. Then repeat the exercise using the right hand, again at all octaves on the piano. Advanced students can try playing with hands together and singing.

Composition – Now write an accompaniment to the simple 4 or 6 bar melody composed in step 15. Make sure that it isn't too complicated.

Small Animal Tiles/Wooden Animals – Place the tiles or wooden animals appropriately on the keyboard and the staves. Now that the child knows all of the notes please explain to him/her that the animals "Cat, Dog, Egg, Fish, Goose, Ant, Bird" keep repeating both on the staves and on the keyboard in different pitches.

Musical Pieces – Sing and play the melody of "All Over the Universe" (page 44), playing bars 1 to 3 with the right hand, bars 4 to 7 with the left hand and bar 8 with the right hand. Sing the left hand melody an octave higher if necessary, as is done on the CD. Do not forget to talk about this picture. In general children are fascinated by it and love to talk about it.

STEP 17

Sung Finger Exercise – Play hands *separately* and sing:

♩ ♩ ♩ ♩ ♩

    Cat   Dog   Egg   Fish   Goose

First play this with the right hand at all octaves on the piano. Then repeat the same exercise using the left hand, again at all octaves on the piano. If the child is ready then you can vary the melody, rhythm or hands.

Musical Pieces – Play and sing "Jingle Bells" (page 43). This music is repeated. The first time you play the two bars that have the number 1 above them and the second time you play the two bars that have a number 2 above them instead. If the child loves this piece then try to get him/her to play it by heart. He/she should sing the animal names.

Composition – Try to play your composition with hands together, singing the animal names in the melody whilst you play.

Rhythm Exercises – Tap page 40, numbers 3 and 4.

Musical Pieces – Play "All Over the Universe" (page 44) hands together. Do this first whilst counting and then whilst singing the animal names. As you play either sing the melody using beats or the animal names.

Small Animal Tiles/Wooden Animals – Place the tiles or wooden animals on both the keyboard and on the staves in the appropriate positions. Once again make sure that the child understands clearly the repeating pattern of the animals on both the keyboard and the staves.

The Echo Game – Play the echo game with Cat, Dog, Egg, Fish and Goose. This is usually quite hard for the students – miss out one or two notes if necessary, or make the order of the notes simple (that is do not use tricky intervals). You can again use the wooden animals or tiles.

Section 4 – Some Helpful Tips to Make Things Easier, in Particular for the Very Young Child

In some cases it is possible to use the Dogs and Birds method with children younger than four. Parental help is usually essential in these situations and if the child is having lessons it is good if the parent attends. This section contains further tips that will help when teaching very young children. They are also useful for slightly older children, if they are having difficulty with specific aspects of the approach. In particular, the small animal tiles and coloured staves are important when working with older children as well. They constitute a "board game", which the children love to play, and which speeds up note recognition and memorizing significantly.

Further use of the Small Animal Tiles and Coloured Staves

The animal tiles and coloured staves are especially useful for the very young. There is an animal for every white key on a full size piano keyboard. The child can therefore use the tiles to find all the Dogs on the keyboard (placing the Dog tiles in appropriate positions), and similarly for the other animals when you introduce them. The animal tiles can also be placed on the coloured staves, with Blu-Tack (or an equivalent adhesive putty). Since the front and back "covers" of the staves show the correct positions of the animals both on the keyboard and the lines of the staves children can turn over the board to check their answers. Also, by looking at the covers parents can easily see the correct positions, even if they have limited musical experience.

Sometimes it is important to emphasize to the child that you read music horizontally and not vertically. For example only the Dog can sit just below the first line on the treble clef. This can be demonstrated very easily if you have a whole set of Dogs. Ask your child to place 5 or so Dogs in a row in the correct position on the staves. They should then play them on the piano and sing. This exercise can be repeated as you add more animals. The child can also use the tiles and staves to make up new finger exercises to try on the piano, and to compose new songs.

Using the Coloured Staves on the Piano in Place of the Score

In some cases it is possible to help very young children to learn to read music by turning the tiles and staves into a musical score. You can "compose" music in front of their eyes for them to play. This helps in particular with learning the position of the notes on the staves. The staves can be placed on the piano instead of the music. Very young children can often read more easily from this "score" than they can from the music in the tutor book. Form a simple melody (for example with Dogs and Birds) using the tiles, and stick them onto the staves with Blu-Tack. Then ask the child to play the melody on the keyboard and sing. You can then form another tune and ask the child to play and sing that. This technique can be very helpful, especially with the very young. You can continue to use this approach as you compose finger exercises and pieces.

Since the tiles are black on the back they can be turned over when the child is confident of the position of the note. This in some sense simulates moving from the animal note edition to the blank note edition of the book.

A Variation on the Listening Game for the Very Young

A very young child might not be able to point out the position of the Dog and the Bird on the large set of staves when you play the ear-training games. This may happen because he/she does not understand the concept of the exercise. If this is the case then you should place a Dog tile or wooden Dog in his/her right hand and a Bird tile or wooden Bird in his/her left. Ask the child to cover up the animals with his/her fingers. When you play a Dog or a Bird, the child should either raise up the appropriate hand or open his/her fingers to expose the animal he/she recognizes by the sound. You can say that the Dog and Bird are talking with each other. The child is therefore indicating which of them is speaking at a given time.

Various Techniques to Help with Rhythm

If your child is very young (three years old or younger) it may be that he/she doesn't understand the difference between a Car and a Big-Car.

In that case you can use small rectangles of white and black paper to symbolize minims/half notes and crotchets/quarter notes. Make the white pieces of paper twice as long but the same width as the black pieces of paper. Form a series of long and short notes using the pieces of paper. Then "tap" this series on the keyboard, together with the child, saying aloud "Short Short Long | Long Short Short", for example. Hold the child's hands as he/she "taps" with his/her palms as explained in step 2. It is better to tap a long note than to clap it since you can make the note sound for two beats. You can also ask the child to compose some rhythmic phrases using the pieces of paper and then tap and say them as earlier. If you have access to a photocopier you can produce black paper by opening the lid and pressing "copy".

Another trick is to ask the child to "bark" the rhythm. The really very young child might find counting or using vehicles too hard, yet they might well be able to bark the beat:
    "woof woof woof woof | woof woof woof woof ".
Combine this with clapping whilst barking a steady beat continuously. Hold a crotchet/quarter note for one woof, a minim/half note for two and a semibreve/whole note for four.

When teaching the child to tap the rhythm exercises hands together you can call out various words to aid them as they tap, for example Red, Blue, Both, Hold.

Helping the Child by Pointing out Notes with Your Fingers
When your child starts to play the musical pieces, it can be very helpful if at the beginning you use your fingers to point out the notes on the musical score as he/she plays. This technique is even more beneficial when tapping the rhythm exercises. If you count aloud (SLOWLY) and follow the notes from left to right, using your left hand, you can use your middle finger (maybe marked with red) to help read the top line and your index finger (maybe marked blue) to help with the bottom line. The easiest way to describe this is to say that the fingers should "walk" along the music (from left to right) with the middle finger touching the top notes and the index finger touching the bottom notes

when they should be tapped. In general at any given point in Book 1 the rhythm exercises are more complicated than the pieces and may require more practice. This is because the rhythm exercises are a preparation for later pieces. You can also help with the musical pieces by pointing with a pencil. You and the child should hold the pencil together and point as you sight-sing the piece.

Walking on the Staves

Another way of helping the young child to remember the positions of the notes on the staves is to allow them to walk on the large set of staves. This can work for very young children – and they love to do it. Or you can make your own stave with five strips of ribbon, for example, taped to the floor. As you play notes on the piano get your child to step on the appropriate line or space. It is best to teach the lines first because it is easier for the child to walk on one line without touching any other. To start with play Egg Egg Egg Egg on the piano and ask your child to step on the first line. Then play Goose Goose Goose Goose. After that play Egg Goose Egg Goose ... You should always make sure that your child sings with the steps. You can also use the animal names to label the lines. For example you can call the first line in the treble clef the Egg line and the second line the Goose line.

An Alternative Order for the Pieces in Book 1

Very young children sometimes have difficulty playing with both hands simultaneously (i.e. hands together). If this is the case then it is recommended to change the order of the pieces. This situation first occurs in the piece "Hands Together". Avoid these pieces and continue playing the pieces where this does not occur – "Stick and Hat Stomp" (page 34), "Old MacDonald" (page 38) and "Jingle Bells" (page 43). You can also play "Aquarium" (page 39) and "Transposition" (page 41), which only have simultaneous notes in the last bar. In this way the child will learn the Cat and the Fish. Meanwhile focus systematically on the rhythm exercises (which are extremely important for helping the child to play pieces hands together) and on playing finger exercises hands together. One common problem is that if a child plays two notes simultaneously on the keyboard (by putting the fingers down at the same time) he/she then wants to remove them from the keyboard at the same time. One way to avoid this tendency (and to help the child to "feel" what it is like to play two notes at once) is to create special finger exercises. For example ask the child to play a long Dog in the right (red) hand and keep it held down whilst playing other notes freely with the left (blue) hand. Start the Dog before playing the other notes. Or you can start by playing a long Goose in the left hand and improvise freely above it with the right hand. The key to being able to play hands together well is to do lots of finger exercises. You can link this strongly with composition, possibly using the small animal tiles and coloured staves.

Once the child has become proficient in doing rhythm exercises and finger exercises hands together you can then work through the pieces on pages 29 to 31, 33, 35, 37, 42 and 44.

This highlights the importance of the rhythm exercises. As mentioned in section 2 very young children often find the rhythm exercises harder than the pieces, and there could be a tendency to miss them out. Please avoid this tendency since mastering the rhythm exercises is vital in developing a good sense of beat and pulse.

The Transition From Animal Notes to Blank Notes
Sometimes children are reluctant to change from the Animal Notes to the Blank Notes Edition. It is possible for the child to play the pieces just using the animals, without fully understanding the position of the animal on the staves, although using the tiles or wooden animals, and staves should help with this. However, if you have progressed towards the end of the book and the child is still having difficulties, you can start to teach steps and skips. Throughout Book 1 only the white notes on the keyboard are used. In this case a step is the distance between a line and a space on the staves, which corresponds to moving from one white key to the adjacent white key, and a skip is the distance between two lines or two spaces on the staves, which corresponds to jumping over the adjacent key to the next nearest white key. Examples of skips are moving up from Bird to Dog or moving down from Bird to Goose.

The child should know by this stage that moving up on the staves corresponds to going to the right on the keyboard and moving down on the staves corresponds to going to the left.

At first you should practise with your child just on the keyboard. The connection with the notation will come naturally at a later stage. The Teacher/Parent should play a Dog, say "Step Up" then play an Egg; say "Step Up" then play a Fish; say "Step Up" then play a Goose. Continue slowly and systematically in this manner, asking your child to repeat what you are doing. Gradually he/she will begin to understand the process, and soon you will be able to teach "Step Down". Once the child has mastered this, you can try something else, for example a skip, or repeating the same note. Introduce everything very slowly, making sure your child understands one concept completely before introducing the next.

Bringing a Toy Animal or Doll to Visit the Animals
A very good stimulus for a young child is for him/her to bring a favourite toy, for example a rabbit or a mouse, or a favourite doll to "visit" the musical animals. This can be a finger puppet or cuddly toy. Or the child could bring a toy car or bicycle for the animals to ride. You can say, "Let's take your toy to visit the Dog. Where does the Dog live?" Knock on the piano (as if knocking on the door of the house) and then get the child to put a Dog tile or wooden Dog on a "D" and bring the toy to it. Or go to visit the Fish. Does the Fish have enough water in his tank? You can do a similar thing with the staves rather than the keyboard. These games can work well, and serve to fire the child's imagination.

A Copying Game
Possibly after a few weeks of improvisation the child would like to try something new. The copying game can be introduced as a replacement for improvisation. You should get the child to play groups of 4 to 6 notes together on the keyboard using open palms. Play with both the right and left hands and play from the shoulder – this is excellent for

learning to play with free arms. You should play all the notes simultaneously. This may be noisy, but the children love it!

First the parent or teacher should play and the child should copy. Then, after a while, switch around, so that the child plays first and the parent or teacher copies. Just vary what is played, for example a series of long and short sounds, or loud and soft, or high and low. Talk about what you are playing. You can also mix the elements as the child gets more proficient. This is a good exercise for improving concentration and memory, as well teaching many elements of music.

Playing the Echo Game without Notation

You can start ear-training without using any notation. This will become useful later on for improvisation or for playing a well-known melody by ear.

Play a simple sequence of Dogs and Birds on the piano, for example Bird Dog Bird Bird or Dog Bird Bird Dog. Ask the child to play and sing it back straight away. If he/she finds this easy then you can add rhythm as well to this echo game, for example Long-Dog Long-Dog Short-Bird Short-Bird Long-Dog. Gradually you can add more and more notes, but make sure that the child can always perform the exercise easily. As long as the child is successful he/she will want to do more and more of these exercises. You need not worry about which fingers to use. Let the child do whatever he/she is comfortable with.

Although you may need to give a lot of help initially, as your child becomes more confident you can make the phrases longer and make the melodies more complicated.

Another Variation on the Listening Game and the Echo Game

Ask your child to make up and play a simple melody. You then need to play this melody back. If you deliberately make some mistakes when you play it back your child will have great fun spotting these.

Making use of New Technology

If the child's parents have a smartphone or tablet then it is good to download a mini-piano. The children can then do ear-training or practise the echo game in the park, in the car, when waiting for something, or even during their holidays. There are many options, for example "Pianist" for the iPhone or "Pianist Pro" for the iPad.

Section 5 – Important Notes for Parents

Hand Position and Posture
When playing the keyboard it is important to work towards a correct hand position and good posture from the start, thereby avoiding getting into bad habits.

The extent to which you can achieve a correct hand position depends on the child. If the child's hands are ready to form a proper hand position you should encourage this, however please do not be too strict. For children with less well-developed hands it is important that they strike the keys in a comfortable way.

Ask the child to hold his/her head in his/her hands like a ball. This should produce the correct hand position with curved fingers. When playing use the tips of the fingers and the side of the thumb, with the palm facing down.

You should always try to get the best out of the child. Therefore if the child can hold his/her hand firmly with curved fingers then always remind him/her to do so. However if the child is having problems with pitch, rhythm, sitting or reading the symbols then concentrate on these first and do not be too rigid about getting a correct hand position. HOWEVER make sure that all the fingers are above the keys and the palms are facing down, not sideways, and that the arms are free. You should make sure that the elbows are comfortably far from the body and that the shoulders are not pushed up. You should avoid any tension in the child. His/her heels should be on the floor – put something firm underneath if the child's legs are too short. He/she must not cross his/her legs. It is also important that the child should always sit with a straight back and should not push his/her wrists up or down when playing. The lower arm should be level with or slightly above the keyboard.

Musical Notation

The Names of the Notes

In music a note of a certain pitch is given a name and conventionally letters are used. There are 88 keys (both black and white) on a full size piano, corresponding to 88 different pitches, however there are *not* 88 different names. The notes are divided into groups, with 12 pitches (seven white keys and five black keys) in each group. Look at the keyboard and find this repeating pattern of keys. In Book 1 only white notes are used and seven names (C, D, E, F, G, A, B) are needed to describe them. Therefore each letter will occur more than once on the keyboard. This same pattern of white notes is repeated all the way along the keyboard.

Since young children find it difficult to remember letters, in Dogs and Birds the notes are represented by animal symbols – with which the child should be very familiar already. The seven names now become Cat, Dog, Egg, Fish, Goose, Ant, Bird. Each animal has specific places both on the keyboard and on the musical staves (the sets of five lines used to notate music). The positions the animals (or letters) occupy on the keyboard is shown on the back page of Book 1. For example, the first note that the child should learn is D – the Dog. The Dog "lives" between the two black keys on the keyboard. This is by far the easiest white note for the child to recognize, which is why the method starts here.

Immediately to the left of the Dog on the keyboard is the Cat – C, and the C that is closest to the centre of the keyboard is called "middle C". In this book the position of middle C on the musical staves is right in the centre of the two sets of 5 lines. The best example of this can be found on page 38 – "Old MacDonald".

Beats and Note Lengths

The speed of a piece of music is determined by the beat, which is the basic unit of time. You should establish the beat before you start to play a piece, as you will hear on the CD. The beats must be even all through the piece. You should ask the student to play/sing/count with a beat corresponding to a time interval of about one second, as you will hear on the CD.

In music the length of a note is as important as its pitch. The lengths of notes are measured in beats. Four different note symbols are used in this book. The longest note is the white note without a stem. This is called a semibreve in the UK and a whole note in the US. In all of the music in this book the semibreve has a length of 4 beats. The white notes with the stems (minims/half notes) are 2 beats long. Putting a "dot" immediately after a note increases its length by half as much again. Therefore a dotted minim has a length of 3 beats rather than 2. The black notes (crotchets/quarter notes) have a length of 1 beat. The lengths of the notes are represented pictorially on the back page of Book 1.

The Octave
The most important musical interval (the difference in pitch between two sounds) is the octave. For example C to the next C (above or below), or D to the next D etc., is an interval of one octave. In order to play the pieces in Book 1 your keyboard should have at least three octaves – it may have as many as seven and a half.

The Musical Staves and the Clefs
A typical line of keyboard music consists of two staves, each of five horizontal lines, joined together. See for example the music on page 3. In all of the music in this book the right hand should be used to play the notes on the upper staff (or stave) and the left hand should be used to play the notes on the lower staff. Notes between the staves should be played with the right hand if the stem on the note points up and with the left hand if the stem points down.

The symbols at the start of each line of music are the treble and bass clefs. The treble clef is on the upper staff and the bass clef on the lower. The clefs are important in that they determine where the animals sit on the staves. For example the Dog sits under the bottom line when the treble clef is used (i.e. the upper staff for the music in this book) and the Bird sits above the top line when the bass clef is used. Hand symbols are used to show which hand should play the notes on a particular staff. These hand symbols are not conventional and will not be found in ordinary music.

Bar Lines
All music is divided into short sections called bars (or measures in the US), each containing a well-defined number of beats. Most of the pieces in this book have four beats in a bar, however later on some music with three beats in a bar is introduced. The number of beats in a bar is important since it determines the character of the piece. For example a march has four beats in a bar whereas a waltz has three beats. The vertical lines separating notes that you can see in both the rhythm exercises and the musical pieces are called bar lines.

Repeat Marks
The two vertical lines with dots (which can occur anywhere on a stave) are repeat marks (see for example page 3). They signify that the phrase has to be repeated. If the music is not to be repeated the piece will end with double vertical lines, but without the dots (for example on page 24).

First and Second Time Bars
In "Jingle Bells" on page 43 the music is repeated with an alternative ending. First the music is played through to the end of the bars labelled 1 but after repeating, these two bars are replaced by the bars labelled 2. To make it easier for the child you can call these the first and second exits. For example you can leave a house by the front door or the back door (but not by both at once).

Da Capo al Fine
In "Old MacDonald" on page 38 the first line is repeated before going on to the second line. The "Da Capo al Fine" marking means that the student should go back to the beginning of the piece and play until the "Fine" marking. This time he/she should not repeat the first line.

Section 6 – Additional Explanatory Notes for Teachers

Rests and Time Signatures

It was decided not to use musical rests in Book 1 since it is harder for the child to keep the beat if rests are included. They are introduced in Book 2. In addition time signatures are not used. At this stage they are an unnecessary complication for the students.

Quavers

Throughout Book 1 quavers have been avoided. In order to establish a good technique on the piano it is important never to play too fast initially and children tend to rush quavers. Their lengths are shown on the back cover of Book 2, however this is the only reference to them there.

Quavers are introduced in Dogs and Birds: Nursery Rhymes and Famous Melodies. Here both the rhythms and the speeds of the pieces are well-known. It is appropriate to use quavers in this case.

Finger Numbers

Finger numbers are not used in Book 1. They are introduced immediately at the start of Book 2. In the Dogs and Birds approach the child learns to associate the notes with animal symbols rather than finger numbers. If the child learns to associate notes with finger numbers (as is the case with most books) this can later cause reading problems as more than ten notes are introduced. This problem is avoided completely by using the animal symbols.

Group Teaching

The different elements discussed here can easily be carried out in a group context. Children can learn to sing and play the keyboard together. A great advantage of the Dogs and Birds method for group teaching is that animal notes and blank notes editions can be used in parallel as required, depending on the abilities of each of the children. You can also cater for those with learning difficulties by putting the animal stickers on the keys.

Section 7 – CD Tracks and Credits

Tracks

Track 1 of the CD contains an introduction which is followed by examples of sung finger exercises, simple improvisation exercises and the echo game. Each subsequent track number on the CD corresponds to the identical page number in Book 1. For example the rhythm exercises on page 2 of the book are on track 2, and "Playground" and "By the Lake", which are on page 3 of the book are on track 3. This makes it very easy to find any musical piece or rhythm exercise in the book – just go to the track that corresponds to the page you are on.

Credits

Keyboard: Elza Lusher
Voice: Ameera Gill
Recording and mixing: Jeff Ross